FOREVER
VIENNA

WISE PUBLICATIONS
part of The Music Sales Group
London/New York/Paris/Sydney/Copenhagen/Berlin/Madrid/Hong Kong/Tokyo

PUBLISHED BY
WISE PUBLICATIONS
14/15 BERNERS STREET, LONDON W1T 3LJ, UK.

EXCLUSIVE DISTRIBUTORS:
MUSIC SALES LIMITED
DISTRIBUTION CENTRE, NEWMARKET ROAD,
BURY ST EDMUNDS, SUFFOLK IP33 3YB, UK.

MUSIC SALES PTY LIMITED
20 RESOLUTION DRIVE, CARINGBAH, NSW 2229, AUSTRALIA.

ORDER NO. AM1000439
ISBN 978-1-84938-518-3

THIS BOOK © COPYRIGHT 2010 WISE PUBLICATIONS,
A DIVISION OF MUSIC SALES LIMITED.

UNAUTHORISED REPRODUCTION OF ANY PART OF THIS PUBLICATION BY
ANY MEANS INCLUDING PHOTOCOPYING IS AN INFRINGEMENT OF COPYRIGHT.

MUSIC ARRANGED BY VASCO HEXEL.
MUSIC PROCESSED BY PAUL EWERS MUSIC DESIGN.

PRINTED IN THE EU.

WWW.MUSICSALES.COM

YOUR GUARANTEE OF QUALITY:

AS PUBLISHERS, WE STRIVE TO PRODUCE EVERY BOOK
TO THE HIGHEST COMMERCIAL STANDARDS.

THE MUSIC HAS BEEN FRESHLY ENGRAVED AND THE BOOK HAS BEEN
CAREFULLY DESIGNED TO MINIMISE AWKWARD PAGE TURNS AND TO MAKE
PLAYING FROM IT A REAL PLEASURE. PARTICULAR CARE HAS BEEN GIVEN
TO SPECIFYING ACID-FREE, NEUTRAL-SIZED PAPER MADE FROM PULPS
WHICH HAVE NOT BEEN ELEMENTAL CHLORINE BLEACHED.

THIS PULP IS FROM FARMED SUSTAINABLE FORESTS AND
WAS PRODUCED WITH SPECIAL REGARD FOR THE ENVIRONMENT.

THROUGHOUT, THE PRINTING AND BINDING HAVE BEEN PLANNED
TO ENSURE A STURDY, ATTRACTIVE PUBLICATION WHICH SHOULD GIVE
YEARS OF ENJOYMENT.

IF YOUR COPY FAILS TO MEET OUR HIGH STANDARDS, PLEASE INFORM US
AND WE WILL GLADLY REPLACE IT.

The Blue Danube

Composed by Johann Strauss

Arranged by André Rieu & Gerardus Huijts

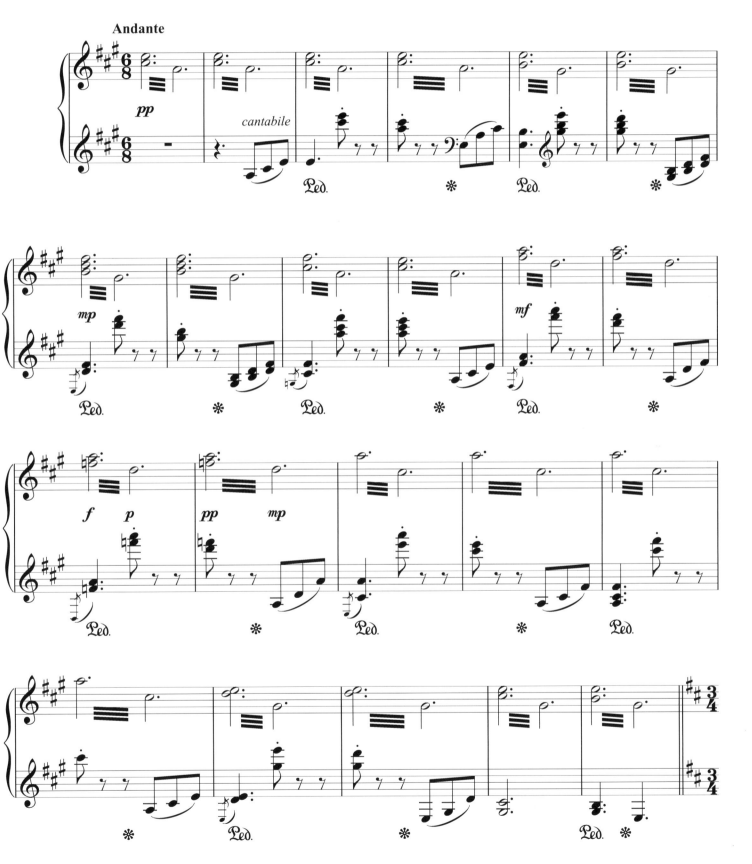

© Copyright 1995 Universal Music Publishing Limited.
All rights in Germany administered by Universal Music Publ. GmbH.
All Rights Reserved. International Copyright Secured.

Tempo di Valse (♩ = *c.* 165)

Radetzky March

Composed by Johann Strauss
Arranged by André Rieu & Jo Huijts

© Copyright 1996 Universal Music Publishing Limited.
All rights in Germany administered by Universal Music Publ. GmbH.
All Rights Reserved. International Copyright Secured.

The Second Waltz

Music by Dmitrij Shostakovich
Arranged by André Rieu

© Copyright 1997 Boosey & Hawkes Music Publishers Limited.
All Rights Reserved. International Copyright Secured.

rall.

a tempo

22

24

Voices Of Spring

Composed by Johann Strauss
Arranged by André Rieu

© Copyright 1995 Universal Music Publishing Limited.
All rights in Germany administered by Universal Music Publ. GmbH.
All Rights Reserved. International Copyright Secured.

Strauss & Co

Composed by Johann Strauss II, Franz Lehar & Emmerich Kalman
Arranged by André Rieu & Jo Huijts

© Copyright 2000 Universal Music Publishing Limited (66.67%)/Copyright Control (33.33%).
All rights in Germany administered by Universal Music Publ. GmbH.
All Rights Reserved. International Copyright Secured.

Bolero

Music by Maurice Ravel
Arranged by André Rieu

© Copyright 2009 by André Rieu Publishing BV
subpublished worldwide ex Benelux by Rolf Budde Musikverlag Gmbh, Berlin.
Administered in the UK & EIRE by Chelsea Music Publishing Company Limited.

43

getting increasingly louder on each repeat

Perpetuum Mobile

Composed by Johann Strauss
Arranged by André Rieu & Gerardus Huijts

© Copyright 1999 PolyGram Music Publishing Limited.
All Rights Reserved. International Copyright Secured.

Repeat ad lib.

Wine, Women And Song

Music by Johann Strauss
Arranged by André Rieu

Tempo di Valse (♩ = c. 160)

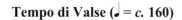

© Copyright 2009 by André Rieu Publishing BV
subpublished worldwide ex Benelux by Rolf Budde Musikverlag Gmbh, Berlin
Administered in the UK & EIRE by Chelsea Music Publishing Company Limited.
All Rights Reserved. International Copyright Secured.

Thunder And Lightning Polka

Music by Johann Strauss
Arranged by André Rieu

© Copyright 1995 Universal Music Publishing Limited.
All rights in Germany administered by Universal Music Publ. GmbH.
All Rights Reserved. International Copyright Secured.

Carnaval de Venise

Composed by Verdi, Strauss, Lehar, Waldteufel & Rosas
Arranged by André Rieu & Jo Huijts

© Copyright 1996 Universal Music Publishing Limited.
All rights in Germany administered by Universal Music Publ. GmbH.
All Rights Reserved. International Copyright Secured.

Tempo di Valse ♩ = 185

Vienna Blood

Composed by Johann Strauss

Arranged by André Rieu & Gerardus Huijts

Allegro moderato

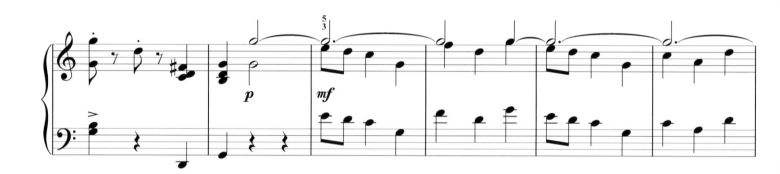

Andante

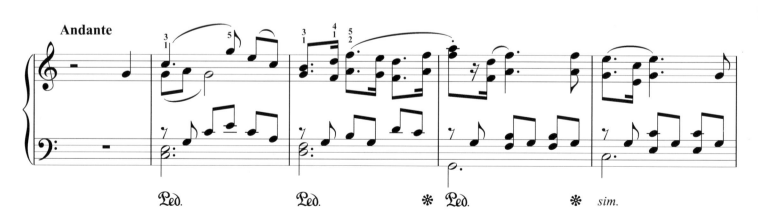

© Copyright 1995 Universal Music Publishing Limited.
All rights in Germany administered by Universal Music Publ. GmbH.
All Rights Reserved. International Copyright Secured.

Tempo di Valse

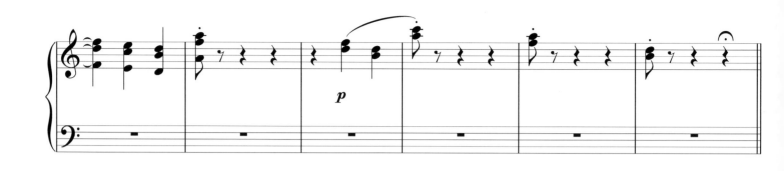

1.

2.

meno mosso

Tempo di Valse

poco accel.

82

The Gypsy Baron

Music by Johann Strauss
Arranged by André Rieu

© Copyright 2009 KPM Music Limited.
All Rights Reserved. International Copyright Secured.

The Merry Widow Waltz

Music by Franz Lehar

© Copyright 1934 Chappell Music Limited.
All Rights Reserved. International Copyright Secured.

89

On Holiday

Composed by Strauss
Arranged by André Rieu

© Copyright 2010 Copyright Control.
All Rights Reserved. International Copyright Secured.

92

Vilja Song

Music by Franz Lehar
Arranged by André Rieu

© Copyright 1934 Chappell Music Limited.
All Rights Reserved. International Copyright Secured.

You Are My Heart's Delight

Music by Franz Lehar
Arranged by André Rieu

© Copyright 2009 Glocken Verlag Limited.
All Rights Reserved. International Copyright Secured.

Strauss Party

Composed by Strauss, Offenbach, Lehar, Suppe & Dostal
Arranged by André Rieu & Jo Huijts

© Copyright 2009 Universal Music Publishing Limited.
All rights in Germany administered by Universal Music Publ. GmbH.
All Rights Reserved. International Copyright Secured.